D1085441

Pope John Paul II

Pope John Paul II conducts an outdoor mass during a 1984 visit to Switzerland.

JUNIOR ■ WORLD ■ BIOGRAPHIES

Pope John Paul II

JAY WILSON

CHELSEA JUNIORS

a division of CHELSEA HOUSE PUBLISHERS

Chelsea House Publishers
EDITOR-IN-CHIEF: Remmel Nunn
MANAGING EDITOR: Karyn Gullen Browne
PICTURE EDI┌─┐ ‥ ‥ n G. Allen
ART DIRECTC J ┊pes
ASSISTANT A ▮ OR: Howard Brotman
MANUFACTUI Joh CTOR: Gerald Levine
SYSTEMS MAi c.1 ιdsey Ottman
PRODUCTION : Marie Claire Cebrián

JUNIOR WORLD BIOGRAPHIES

SENIOR EDITOR: Kathy Kuhtz

Staff for POPE JOHN PAUL II
ASSOCIATE EDITOR: Philip Koslow
COPY EDITOR: Daniel O'Connell
EDITORIAL ASSISTANT: Danielle Janusz
PICTURE RESEARCHER: Sandy Jones
SENIOR DESIGNER: Marjorie Zaum
COVER ILLUSTRATION: Bill Donahey

First Printing

1   3   5   7   9   8   6   4   2

Library of Congress Cataloging-in-Publication Data
Wilson, Jay (K. Jay)
    Pope John Paul II/Jay Wilson.
        p.   cm.—(Junior world biographies)
    Includes bibliographical references and index.
    Summary: A biography of the Polish cardinal who became the first non-
Italian to be elected pope since 1523.
    ISBN   0-7910-1758-3
    1. John Paul II, Pope, 1920–   —Juvenile literature.   2. Popes—
Biography—Juvenile literature.   [1. John Paul II, Pope, 1920–   .   2. Popes.]
I. Title.   II. Series.
BX1378.5.W554   1992   91-39384
282'.092—dc20   CIP
[B]   AC

Contents

A view of St. Peter's Square and the Vatican in Rome. On October 16, 1978, more than 100,000 people waited in the square while the cardinals elected Karol Cardinal Wojtyła the first Polish pope in history.

1

A Polish Pope

On the evening of October 16, 1978, 100,000 people filled St. Peter's Square in Rome, Italy. They were gathered in front of the *Vatican*, the palatial headquarters of the *Roman Catholic church*. Many of them had been waiting for two days. A new *pope* was to be chosen to head the church, and the event had created suspense and excitement for Catholics and non-Catholics alike.

As the crowd waited, a puff of white smoke rose from a chimney of the Vatican. This was the age-old signal that a pope had been chosen. Then an elderly *cardinal*—one of the church officials ranking just below the pope—walked out onto the balcony of the palace. As the crowd cheered, the red-robed cardinal announced that there was indeed a new pope: "He is Cardinal Karol Wojtyła, who has taken the name of John Paul II."

When they heard the name, the people in the square were amazed. For the past 455 years, every pope had been Italian. Karol Wojtyła (pronounced voy-TEE-wuh) was Polish. The crowd was eager for a sight of the man who had inspired such a break with the past.

Finally, at 7:22 P.M., Karol Cardinal Wojtyła, now Pope John Paul II, appeared on the balcony. He was a solidly built man in his late fifties, with a square-jawed, intelligent face. Many in the crowd were surprised when he began to speak in almost perfect Italian. Addressing the people in the square as "dearly beloved brothers and sisters," he told them that the cardinals had called him "from a far country—distant and yet always close because of our communion in faith and Christian tradition. I was afraid to accept this choice, but I did so in a spirit of humility and obedience to our Lord." The crowd roared with approval.

As pope, John Paul II became the head of the Roman Catholic church. From the Vatican, his official residence, the pope governs the spiritual life of the worldwide community of Catholics, who number more than 900 million. Once chosen, a pope remains in office until he dies. Then a new pope is elected by the cardinals, 120 senior priests from around the world.

For nearly 2,000 years the structure of the Catholic church has remained unchanged. The pope directs the cardinals; the cardinals direct the *bishops*; the bishops govern the churches and advise the priests, who guide the worshipers. This structure is older than any other government on earth, and it came about in a remarkable way.

According to the Catholic religion, Jesus

Christ, before his death, gave his disciple St. Peter power to rule the church in Christ's name. St. Peter became the first pope, and the holy power given to him has been passed on to all the popes after him. Catholics believe that the pope is Christ's representative on earth. He guides the church not merely by his own thoughts; he is also inspired by the spirit of God. Catholics believe that the pope speaks with the authority of the redeemer of the human race, Jesus Christ. When they respect and honor him, they respect and honor Christ.

Because Rome has been the center of the church for most of its history, it is not surprising that popes have usually been Italian. Until the election of Cardinal Wojtyła in 1978, no pope had ever come from Poland, a Slavic country in eastern Europe. Although most Poles were Catholics, the country had been ruled since 1945 by the *Communist party*, which officially denied the existence of God. The Polish Communist government allowed Catholics to worship but sharply restricted the involvement of priests in any aspect of daily life outside their churches. Karol Wojtyła had served as a priest, a bishop, and a cardinal under these conditions. He had led Polish Catholics through years of dictatorship and harsh poverty. The cardinals who elected him pope believed that the talents he had shown in Poland would benefit the world community of Catholics.

Beginning in the late 1970s, Poland had often been in the headlines and on the nightly TV news. Around the world, people watched the rise of the *Solidarity* movement, which began among the shipyard workers of the port city of Gdansk. Solidarity is a union of workers who rejected unfair orders from their government bosses and insisted on better working conditions. The workers demanded their rights to safety on the job, fair wages, and health care as well as a voice in the way their factories were run. To the amazement of the world, Solidarity's efforts led to the downfall of the Polish Communist government. The people then chose Lech Walesa (LEK vuh-LEN-suh), a worker who was the leader of Solidarity, to serve as president of a new, democratic Poland. By 1991 the democratic movement that had triumphed in Poland had spread throughout Eastern Europe.

By electing a Polish cardinal to the *papacy* in 1978, the cardinals announced to the world that the Catholic church supported the spirit of change. In Poland the news touched off an explosion of joy, with people singing and dancing in the streets. To the Polish people, John Paul II was not only Christ's representative in the world but also a special symbol of the spirit of Poland. As a bishop and a cardinal, he had long encouraged the struggle for democracy among his fellow Poles. The Communist government had learned to respect Karol Wojtyła as a man who fought hard for the welfare of the church and for the rights of Polish students to speak and write freely. Impressed by his work in Poland, Catholic officials throughout the world had invited Cardinal Wojtyła to visit their countries. Because he knew more than a dozen foreign languages, he was able to speak directly to the people wherever he went. At every opportunity, he spread the message of freedom for Eastern Europe.

This desire to meet the people did not diminish when Cardinal Wojtyła became Pope John Paul II. Soon after his election, he held a press conference in the Vatican. Reporters who attended were amazed to find the pope plunging into their midst, shaking their hands, and answering their questions with great care. At 58, the youngest of all the 20th-century popes, John Paul II refused to follow the example of earlier popes, who preferred to stay in Rome and preach from the Vatican. Throughout his papacy, he has traveled around the globe, visiting Asia, Africa, and North and South America as well as the nations of Europe. By visiting many poorer countries, especially those in Latin America and Africa, he has called the attention of the world to their plight. In addition, he has been a very active writer, publishing dozens of essays on religious and philosophical topics. There have been few world leaders who can match his energy and productiveness.

Karol Wojtyła, the man who became Pope John Paul II, did not travel the path from Poland to the papacy alone. At each stage of his life, key people—parents, friends, teachers, and others—deeply influenced him. At the same time, he has always been an independent person who makes decisions as honestly as he can, whether they are

Shortly after his election, John Paul II held a news conference at the Vatican. The journalists were delighted when the new pope plunged into their midst, shaking hands, laughing, and eagerly answering all their questions.

popular or not. As pope he has expressed strong opinions about abortion, birth control, the right of priests to marry, and the admission of women to the priesthood. Both Catholics and non-Catholics have often disagreed with the pope and have urged him to change his mind. However, the pope believes that his primary task is to be the conscience of the church, trusting humbly that he will be guided by the spirit of God.

As he directs the church, John Paul II is aware that people must have food, clothing, homes, and jobs. He is equally concerned with the inner life of human beings and with helping to bring them closer to God. John Paul II himself is both a man of action and a man who spends much of his time contemplating God in prayer. In other words, the pope is both a public leader and a very private person. His mission is to bring the private person—the conscience, the human sense of right and wrong—into public life. He sees this mission not only as his own but also as the mission of all people.

*A photograph of young Karol Wojtyła, known as
Lolek, with his mother and father, Emilia and Karol.
Emilia Wojtyła died when Lolek was only eight years
old, but the influence of her kindness and religious
faith remained with him throughout his life.*

2
Lolek

On May 18, 1920, a baby boy was born to Karol and Emilia Wojtyła. The Wojtyłas christened their new son Karol, the Polish equivalent of Charles, although they soon called him by the nickname Lolek. Lolek is a shortened form of Karolek, or Little Karol, or Charlie in English. The family lived in the country market town of Wadowice in southwestern Poland, about 30 miles from the city of Kraków.

The Wojtyłas were simple, hardworking, rural people. They were also devout Catholics.

Little Lolek's father was an officer in the Polish army. His mother's family came from Lithuania, a country to the northeast of Poland on the Baltic Sea. Emilia Wojtyła was a pretty, young woman who had been a schoolteacher before her marriage. She kept house in the family's three-room apartment at 7 Koscielna (Church) Street, where Lolek was born. Emilia Wojtyła was a very religious woman. Even when Lolek was very small, his mother taught him about the Catholic faith, especially about Jesus' mother, Mary, who represents the spirit of love and sympathy. In later life Lolek would call on Mary in moments of great suffering.

When he was seven, Lolek's parents sent him to elementary school. He was a good pupil but not outstanding. His brother Edmund, 15 years older, was also a good student and was beginning to study medicine. Little Lolek enjoyed a secure, ordinary life at home. That security was shattered in April 1929, when Emilia Wojtyła died in childbirth. It was a painful loss for Lolek, almost nine years old, who had been so close to his gentle mother. Many years later, after he had become pope, some of his former schoolmates still remembered his sadness over his mother's death.

Karol Wojtyła had always felt a special fondness for his Lolek, and now father and son grew even closer. It was hard for the military man to keep up a happy home life without his wife. He tried to be strict with Lolek and set up a daily schedule for him, but he left some free time so that Lolek could play soccer with his friends. At this time, Lolek developed what would become a lifelong love of sports. Saddened by his mother's death, however, he was basically a quiet, serious boy. These qualities, uplifted by his father's love, attracted the respect of his teachers and the friendship of his schoolmates.

In 1931, when Lolek was 11, he finished elementary school and enrolled in high school. The next year, tragedy struck again. Lolek's brother, Edmund, who had become a doctor, caught scarlet fever while caring for sick children.

Scarlet fever was a dangerous disease in the years before doctors discovered antibiotics, and Edmund did not recover. On his tombstone are these words: "Edmund died as a victim of his profession in which he had devoted his young life to suffering humanity." He was only 26 years old.

Understandably, this new tragedy drew Lolek and his devoted father even closer. Karol Wojtyła retired from the army to be of more help to his only surviving son. They became everything to each other. As one biographer notes, "He ran the household, cooked for Lolek, washed and mended his clothes. He acted as his son's tutor and coached and coaxed the lad from his first school exercise book through [graduation]. Father and son were inseparable."

Despite the loss of his mother and brother, Lolek's teens were a wonderful period for him. He excelled in high school, taking a special interest in Polish literature and drama. The religious faith he had received from his parents continued to grow. Most of the priests who knew him in these years believed that he was destined for a life in the church.

When Lolek turned 18, he and his father made an important decision. Lolek wanted to go to college, so he and his father made plans to leave Wadowice and move to Kraków. Lolek's destination was the Jagellonian University in Kraków, one of the great old European universities. There he would study literature and theater. The young man had discovered that he loved words and the craft of acting. He would pursue these passions all his life, although not in the ways he imagined when he was a freshman.

Kraków was the artistic capital of Poland. In the early 1930s, it was an exciting city full of beautiful houses, parks, museums, and theaters. And the Jagellonian University, founded in 1364 by the king of Poland, was known throughout the world. Perhaps its most famous graduate was Nicolaus Copernicus (1473–1543), the brilliant Polish astronomer who made one of the greatest scientific discoveries in history. For thousands of years people had believed that the sun revolves around the earth. By proving that the earth revolves around the sun, Copernicus made it possible to understand the stars and planets. More recently, Vladimir Lenin, the father of the 1917 Communist revolution in Russia (later called the Soviet Union), used the Jagellonian's library when he lived in Kraków between 1912 and 1914.

Lolek plunged into college life with zest. He was hoping for a career in the theater. He made friends with other students interested in drama and appeared in many student plays. Away from the university, however, he always kept a certain distance from the other students. He preferred staying home or hiking to going to parties or dancing. He was not afraid of being alone. As one biographer says, "His most intimate and private thoughts were shared only with his father or confined to his regular visits to church." He was popular with his fellow students, yet he was also a serious and private young man.

Karol Wojtyła as a 19-year-old college student at Jagellonian University in Kraków. Wojtyła enjoyed college life, but his studies in literature and drama were cut short by the outbreak of World War II.

During the summer before his sophomore year, Lolek went for the military training that was required of all Polish students. In August he returned to Kraków, eagerly anticipating his new courses in literature and drama. He did not realize that the world was on the eve of a catastrophe.

On September 1, 1939, Germany invaded Poland, and World War II began. Adolf Hitler, the German dictator, used a strategy that he called *blitzkrieg*, or "lightning war." The Nazis swept rapidly through Poland, destroying the outdated Polish forces before they could organize an effective defense. Within a month the government of Poland surrendered. The country would remain under German control for five years.

The German domination of Poland affected every Polish citizen. Germany was ruled by the Nazi party, which believed that the Germans were a "master race" destined to rule the world. All other peoples were considered inferior. As soon as Kraków was taken over, the German military government shut down the universities. Hitler's plans called for the Poles to be used only for "low labor." Thus, there would be no need for anyone to study. "The Poles," declared the Nazi official in charge of Poland, "shall be the slaves of the German Reich [Empire]."

The Nazis arrested and imprisoned most of the Polish *intellectuals* to prevent them from forming a resistance movement. On November 6, 1939, the professors of the Jagellonian University were rounded up and trucked away to concentration camps. The Nazis had set up these camps as centers where people were forced to work, but soon they became vast prisons in which people were tortured and killed. Many of the Jagellonian professors were never heard from again.

The Gestapo, the German secret police, kept a close watch on university students. Young Karol Wojtyła knew he was in danger of being sent to a concentration camp, for many of his friends had already been arrested. His best hope was to get some kind of job, because the Germans were eager to make use of strong workers.

At the beginning of 1940, Karol was hired by the Solway Chemical Works. The company put him to work in a quarry, a huge pit where rocks are taken out of the earth and used to make building materials. He was safe from being arrested, but the work—smashing rocks and loading the pieces onto railroad cars—was exhausting. From this job he was transferred to a more dangerous one, lighting dynamite to blast the rocks in the quarry. After a while, he was taken off this terrifying job and sent to work inside the company's gloomy chemical factory.

While working at the quarry, Karol lived with and supported his father in a humble neighborhood of Kraków. To the outside world he looked like an ordinary workman. In fact, young Karol was now active in the Polish resistance, a secret organization that fought against the Nazis. With a group of other university students, he established a theater group. The actors secretly performed patriotic plays to lift the spirits of the Polish citizens. Both the actors and the audience were taking serious risks. Anyone caught attending such a play would be arrested by the Gestapo. The actors would be executed.

While doing all he could to oppose the Nazis, Karol was also deeply worried about the fate of the Polish Jews. The notorious Auschwitz concentration camp was located near Kraków, and Karol heard rumors that the Germans were killing thousands of Jews there. Although some Poles shared the Nazis' prejudice against the Jews, Karol felt that all Poles were part of the same family. There were important differences between the religions, but Christians and Jews prayed to the same god. Karol felt he had to help. In Kraków and other cities, he worked to find hiding places for Jewish families before the Gestapo could arrest them; in many cases, he helped get Jews passports so that they could leave the country. According to people who knew him at this time, he saved many Jews from certain death.

Karol had grown up in a peaceful world. Now, as a young man, he found himself living

*Nazi troopers round up Polish Jews during the
German occupation of Poland. Although some Poles
were anti-Semitic, Wojtyła believed that all Poles
belonged to the same family; he helped many Jews
avoid imprisonment and death.*

amid the death and destruction of a war. In the midst of this crisis, he lost his last source of comfort and support. In February 1941 his father died. Crushed by grief, Karol spent 12 hours praying over his father's body. At last he came to see his personal loss as part of his country's agony under the Nazi yoke. Alone in the world at the age of 20, he felt a greater kinship with his fellow Poles.

In the depths of tragedy, Karol found a new source of light. His parents had given him their faith, and he had kept it through all his trials. Now he began to have a new vision of the future. "After my father's death," he wrote later, "I was working at the factory and devoting myself as far as the terms of occupation allowed to my taste for literature and drama. My priestly vocation took shape in the midst of all that, like an inner fact of unquestionable clarity. The following year, in the autumn, I knew that I was called."

Father Wojtyła poses with students from the Catholic seminary at Kraków in 1951. Wojtyła was then serving as a parish priest, but he wanted most of all to become a teacher of theology.

3

Priest and Professor

As World War II raged on, the fire for God's calling grew in the young student. A few months after his father's death, Karol decided to change his studies from literature to *theology*, the study of religion. The Nazis had closed the Jagellonian University, but the professors and students continued to hold classes in secret. This project became known as the underground university. Karol Wojtyła enrolled in the university's Department of Theology.

During this troubled period, Karol came under the spiritual influence of two remarkable men. The first was Jan Tyranowski. A tailor by profession, Tyranowski organized the Catholic Youth Organization, which met to discuss religious questions. Tyranowski became Karol's mentor, or spiritual guide. "In his words, in his spirituality, and in the example of a life given entirely to God alone," Karol remembered in later years, "he represented a new world that I did not know."

By the autumn of 1944, the advancing Soviet army was driving the Germans out of Poland, and the Polish Resistance was growing bolder. Nevertheless, Poland was not out of danger, and Karol was fortunate to come under the protection of Adam Sapieha, the archbishop of Kraków. Although an aristocrat (a member of the nobility or upper class), Sapieha was deeply concerned about the poor and the children orphaned by the war. When the Nazis began rounding up and killing thousands of young Polish men, Archbishop Sapieha took action. Courageously, he hid Karol Wojtyła and other students in his official residence in Kraków until the Germans were driven from the city.

Karol completed two years of secret study during the war. When the Jagellonian University reopened at the war's end in 1945, Karol spent two more years finishing his theology studies. On November 1, 1946, he knelt before the archbishop of Kraków, who declared him a priest of the Roman Catholic church. The tasks to which young Father Wojtyła now devoted himself were healing war-torn souls and helping rebuild his native land.

Poland needed teachers to train the next generation of priests, and the archbishop recognized that Wojtyła was just the sort of person who would make an excellent professor at the Kraków *seminary*. (A seminary is a school in which people study to be priests, ministers, or rabbis.) So he sent Father Wojtyła to the Angelicum Institute in Rome for more study. After two years in Rome,

Wojtyła earned his doctor of theology degree in 1948.

When Wojtyła returned to Poland, he found the church in trouble. The Soviet Union had freed Poland from the Germans, but the Soviets would not allow the Poles to go their own way. They set up a Communist government in Poland, a government run by Poles but taking orders from Soviet leaders. At first, the Polish Communists and the church had worked together to rebuild their war-torn country. By the summer of 1948, however, the government and the church were at odds. The church complained about the lack of freedom under Communist rule. The Communists, always opposed to religion, resented the church's hold on the people. The conflict boiled over when Pope Pius XII *excommunicated* (expelled from the church) all members of the Communist party who still considered themselves Catholics. In return the government attacked the church through the newspapers and seized church property. Many priests and worshipers were jailed for church-related activities.

Wojtyła was first assigned to serve as priest in Niegowic (Nyeh-GO-vitz), a small village more than 100 miles from Kraków. This job was a far cry from being a theology professor, but Wojtyła did not complain. On July 18, 1948, he arrived in Niegowic on foot, with nothing but the clothes on his back. Although he was to spend only a year in the village, Wojtyła soon won the hearts of the people with his humility and charity. At Christmastime the girls from the Catholic Youth Organization sewed a feather quilt for their priest because he had almost no personal belongings. Wojtyła accepted the quilt gratefully, then offered it to three of the girls whose mother had recently died.

Despite the mutual love between the parishioners and their young priest, Wojtyła continued to study theology, determined to become a professor. Within a year of Wojtyła's arrival at

Niegowic, the archbishop transferred him to St. Florian's parish in Kraków, the city he considered home.

In 1951, Wojtyła was released from his duties as a parish priest to continue his studies. In two years he earned a doctorate in philosophy to go with his doctorate in theology. By 1953 he was invited to lecture at the Catholic seminary in Kraków. The government had closed the seminary, but it continued to operate secretly. If Wojtyła had been caught lecturing there, he would have been imprisoned. But for him, teaching was worth the risk. It was a genuine part of his vocation as a priest.

Wojtyła was an outstanding teacher and soon became popular with his students. Before long, the directors of the Catholic University of Lublin also noticed his talent. Lublin, 150 miles from Kraków, was the one Catholic university that the Polish Communist government had not closed. The professors at Lublin invited Wojtyła to give several lectures in 1953, and the next year

Taking a break from his duties as a priest, Wojtyła has an open-air shave during a hiking trip in the mountains outside Kraków. Wojtyła's parishioners loved and admired their priest because of his humility and simplicity.

they asked him to join the faculty. By the age of 36, Wojtyła became a full professor and the head of the Institute of Ethics at Lublin. According to Father Feliks Bednarski, a Polish professor at the Angelicum in Rome, "He was . . . a genuine optimist, never happier than when working with young people. . . . The students always loved having him around. When they brought a problem to him, he seemed able to bring a new vision to it."

It was not easy being a person of vision in the Poland of the early 1950s. The government continued to crack down on the church. When the leader of Poland's Catholics, Stefan Cardinal Wyszynski (vuh-SHIN-skee), refused to stop the clergy from criticizing the government, he himself was imprisoned. The situation did not improve until a new generation of Communist leaders took over: They were led by Nikita Khrushchev (krush-CHOF) in the Soviet Union and Władysław Gomulka in Poland. Under the new leaders, thousands of Polish Catholics were released from prison. In December 1956, Gomulka and Wyszynski signed an agreement that guaranteed the Polish church free activity in all areas of public life except political affairs.

During this new period of harmony, when new priests were being trained and new churches were being built, Wojtyła came into his own as a Polish church leader. In 1958, Pope John XXIII chose him to become an auxiliary, or assistant, bishop of Kraków. News of the appointment reached him while he was on a camping trip in the mountains. "The Holy Father has nominated you to become a bishop," he was told. "Will you accept? You know the Holy Father does not like to be turned down."

Wojtyła thought for a moment. "Yes," he said, "providing that I can go back to my camping trip." With a smile and a wave of his hand, he went back to the trails of his beloved countryside.

As archbishop of Kraków, Wojtyła celebrates mass at Wawel Cathedral. Archbishop Wojtyła was not only concerned with religion; under his leadership, the church helped people find medical care and cope with family problems.

4
Vatican II

Bishop Wojtyła brought phenomenal energy to his new job. At 38 he was the youngest bishop in Poland. He visited every parish, chapel, and monastery in the Kraków region. He made a point of meeting every priest. He set up evening discussion groups, inviting *atheists* (those who do not believe in God) and "lapsed" Catholics (those who have stopped attending mass). People who came to the meetings could ask anything they wanted to about faith: Is there a God? Does the soul go on living after the body dies? Through such discussions, Wojtyła tried to draw back those who had drifted away from the church. Yet he also recognized that the Catholic church did not have all the answers. "We and all our fellow men," he said, "are engaged in a search."

In his writings, the new bishop encouraged people to ask themselves, Who am I? and How should I treat other people? In his book *Love and Responsibility*, published in 1960, Wojtyła wrote about the meaning of marriage. In this all-important relationship, he wrote, each partner should think of giving rather than merely seeking satisfaction. To love means to understand that one has a certain responsibility for another person. It is in caring for someone else that one finds joy.

Wojtyła had never lost his love for the theater. He saw no reason why he could not be a bishop and also write plays. Drama provided another perspective on human relationships, on the sorrows and joys of human life. Wojtyła's best-known play, *The Jeweler's Shop*, which also deals with the subject of marriage, was enthusiastically received by Polish audiences. It is still performed today and has even been performed in English.

In 1962, Pope John XXIII called a general council of all the bishops to meet at the Vatican in Rome. It was the first meeting of the world's bishops in almost a century. (The First Vatican Council was held in 1870.) Now the Second Vatican Council, or Vatican II, as it was nicknamed, was going to consider the role of the Catholic church in the modern world. The pope announced that the council would be concerned with the entire human race and its rights to freedom, justice, and happiness. In the course of almost three years of meetings and debates, the church leaders shed new light on how Catholics worship and how they should see themselves in the modern world. Vatican II turned out to be a major event in the history of the church. Catholics are still feeling its effects today—in their church services, which are no longer held in Latin, and in the readiness of the individual churches to involve themselves in community problems.

The Vatican invited Cardinal Wyszynski and 16 Polish bishops to attend the great conference. Shortly before leaving for Rome, Wojtyła spoke in the big cathedral in Kraków. He shared his excitement about Vatican II:

> We are all filled with emotion at this time, each of us in a different way. . . . We all feel—all humanity seems to feel—that this Council will be inspired by the Spirit of Wisdom and of Love, that wisdom and that love which are the greatest hope of humanity today.

Wojtyła believed that the council would bring about a "real change of direction and a transformation at the heart of the Church."

When he joined his 2,500 fellow bishops in the Vatican, Wojtyła felt the thrill of being back in Rome. Only a junior bishop, he felt that he was there to listen to his elders. But when Pope

John XXIII asked the bishops to debate what modern Catholics should believe, Wojtyła was inspired by this spirit of renewal. He decided to speak before the bishops.

Wojtyła expressed his opinion about changing the worship service and about the importance of the Holy Scripture. "Do not hesitate," he declared during one debate, "to call for religious freedom." It was especially important, he continued, "for those of us who live under Communist regimes." In a talk on Vatican Radio (November 26, 1963), he voiced his thoughts on what ordinary Catholics must do to help in the renewal of their faith. Their role is "to make sure that all persons are allowed to reach their full potential, while at the same time allowing for their weaknesses."

During Vatican II the bishops tried to bring the church back to its roots. They reminded themselves and all Catholics that the "church" is not simply the priests and bishops but "all the people of God." They instructed priests to present religion to the people as something that was part of their daily lives. The council also stressed the importance of the community. In their view, the Holy Communion (in which bread and wine are taken to honor the death of Christ) should not

only involve silent conversation between a person and God but also create a sense of spiritual togetherness among all the people at the Mass.

Early one January morning, Rome had a surprise snowfall. An English priest who was at-

The bishops and archbishops of the Catholic church assemble in St. Peter's Basilica for the opening of the Second Vatican Council, in 1962. Wojtyła's contribution to Vatican II convinced many clergymen that he was destined for high office in the church.

47

tending Vatican II, Monsignor Derek Worlock, wrote in his diary that day: "Somehow I waded my way to St. Peter's through the drifts, and was delighted to find the other Europeans and Americans also arriving . . . . There was the splendid sight of the Polish Bishop Wojtyła drying his socks by the stove."

"I remember the occasion well," Worlock told the biographer Mary Craig after Wojtyła became pope. "I can see him coming in, dressed, as he was always dressed, in a cassock [priest's robe], and he was wringing out the bottom of his cassock and taking off his shoes and socks and drying them by the stove, just sitting there with bare feet, completely unconcerned." Monsignor Worlock's words give a perfect snapshot of Wojtyła— relaxed, practical, at home in God's house.

Pope Paul VI (who became pope when Pope John XXIII died in 1963, after the first session of the council) fully embraced the ideas of Vatican II. He recognized Wojtyła as someone who shared his thinking. Sensing the young bishop's new confidence and maturity, Pope Paul named him archbishop of Kraków. At the ceremony in Wawel (VAH-vel) Cathedral, Archbishop Wojtyła spoke to the congregation, which included old neighbors from Wadowice, parishioners from Niegowic and Kraków, teachers from the Kraków seminary and the Catholic University of Lublin, and even a few of his nonreligious friends: "I want to awaken the archdiocese of Kraków to the true meaning of the Council, so that we may bring its teachings into our lives."

When Wojtyła moved into the archbishop's palace, he arrived with his skis slung over his shoulder. Twenty years earlier Wojtyła had entered the same building in the dark of night, a young student hunted by the Nazis. But now it was time to get to work, humbly and practically, to show the people what the church could mean to their life.

*Pope John Paul II dons a sombrero and hugs an
Indian child during his 1979 visit to Mexico. Whereas
other popes had spent most of their time in Rome,
John Paul II traveled the world to express his
concerns for ordinary people and their problems.*

5

A New Force
in the Church

The Second Vatican Council concluded that the modern church should be a "light unto all the people." In other words, Catholics had an obligation to improve the world. Archbishop Wojtyła was eager to answer this call for social action. In Kraków he worked especially hard to help the sick, the disabled, and the dying. He started a new program for these unfortunate people and chose as head of the project a priest who was himself seriously ill. "You are the ideal person for the job," he told the priest. "You know what it is like to be ill and so you will sympathize." The program was a great success.

Wojtyła also created the Family Institute to help Poles with a variety of problems—teenage pregnancy, poverty, juvenile delinquency, alcoholism, and violence in the home. He himself worked part of every day as a counselor in the Family Institute. With all his activities, he put in as many as 20 hours a day. Those who worked with him discovered that he often did two jobs at the same time. For example, he was able to read a report or write a letter while carrying on a conversation with an assistant.

Despite his enormous work load, Wojtyła did find time to relax. Throughout his life he had passionately loved the mountains. During the summer months, he would go for long hikes; during the winter, he went skiing. Those who watched him speed down the slopes often marveled at his fearlessness. One of his skiing companions remembered, "He loved the thrill of it, the sheer danger." Later on, when he became a cardinal, someone asked him whether it was really proper for a cardinal to ski. He replied, "It is not proper for a cardinal to ski badly."

In 1967, Pope Paul VI recognized Wojtyła's energy and achievements by making him a cardinal. He was now among the most powerful men in the church, but he behaved with the same humility toward parishioners and fellow clergymen. For all his humility, though, the Polish government found that he could be a tough opponent. During his tenure as cardinal, he fought for the construction of new churches and stood behind university students when they demanded the right of free speech. As the Solidarity movement grew in power among Poland's workers, people around the world began to look on Cardinal Wojtyła as a symbol of Poland's desire for freedom. He began to travel widely to other nations, impressing Catholics and non-Catholics alike with his grasp of

John Paul II prepares to tackle the slopes of the Italian Alps during a 1984 ski trip. The pope has never lost his love of the outdoors, and he continues to hike and ski whenever his schedule allows.

languages, his intelligence, and his sense of humor.

When Pope Paul VI died in August 1978, Wojtyła traveled to Rome to take part in the election of a new pope. It took the cardinals only a day to make their choice—Albino Cardinal Luciani, who took the name John Paul I. The cardinals had perhaps not realized that the new pope, 65 years old, was in poor health. Burdened by the duties of his office, he died of a stroke hardly more than a month after his election.

When the cardinals gathered once again, observers felt that they would certainly vote for a younger, more vigorous man. Wojtyła had received some votes the previous time, but he himself was sure that the new pope would again be Italian. After all, there had not been a non-Italian pope for 455 years.

To everyone's surprise, the cardinals decided to make history. They first considered three of their Italian brethren but could not agree on one in particular. Franz Cardinal Koenig of Austria then became the favorite. But Koenig declared that he did not wish to be pope and surprised everyone by proposing the name of Karol Cardinal Wojtyła. The voting went on for eight ballots before the crowd in St. Peter's Square learned that Cardinal Wojtyła was indeed the new pope.

It was unusual for a new pope to do more than bless the crowd outside the Vatican. John Paul II insisted on speaking to them. "Today I stand before you," he said in Italian, "to declare our common faith . . . and to set out on a fresh stage of the history of the church, with God's help and that of men and women."

John Paul II made it clear at once that he was dedicated to carrying out the mandate of Vatican II—bringing the church closer to the people. An important part of this mission was the defense of human rights throughout the world. The day after his election as pope, he declared: "We want to stretch out our hands and open our hearts to all people, especially those who are oppressed by injustice or discrimination. . . . We must reach out to them by all possible means . . . so that all people may live a life that is worthy of them."

John Paul II did not intend to stay in Rome and merely talk about human rights. During the 1980s he visited more than 75 nations. He began in 1979 with a trip to Latin America, focusing on Mexico. Having seen for himself the poverty in which many Mexicans lived, the pope declared in a speech that "social justice"—meaning a fair chance for everyone to live a decent life—was necessary if the world was ever to become safe and peaceful. In the past the church had often told poor people to think about God instead of their torn clothes and empty stomachs. John Paul II recognized that it was hard to be a good Christian without the basic necessities of life.

John Paul II's energy and interest in ordinary people made him the most popular pope since John XXIII, who had also spoken out on

John Paul II waves to enthusiastic crowds in Phoenix, Arizona, in 1987. Ever since the attempt on his life in 1981, the pope has been protected by heavy security measures, including a bulletproof covering on the "popemobile."

59

world peace and justice. On May 13, 1981, people throughout the world were horrified to hear that the pope had been shot. Because of his desire to reach the people, John Paul II went out into St. Peter's Square every week. He would stand in the open back of his four-wheel-drive vehicle—known as the "popemobile"—and drive slowly around the square, pausing to bless and speak with anyone who wished to see him. On May 13, a young Turk, Mehmet Ali Agca, made his way through the crowd surrounding the pope, drew a pistol, and fired five shots at the pope. The crowd closed in around the gunman, and security men disarmed him. But two of the bullets had hit John Paul. "Mary, my mother! Mary, my mother!" he cried out, calling upon the Virgin Mary for comfort. Then he collapsed in the back of the popemobile, which sped through the square to a waiting ambulance.

As the world waited in suspense, the pope endured five hours of surgery. Luckily, the bullets had passed right through his body without damaging his stomach, heart, or lungs. Even so, the pope's wounds were serious, and it took John Paul II several months to recover.

Who was Mehmet Ali Agca? Why had he tried to kill the pope? The police learned only that Ali Agca was wanted for murder in Turkey. His own statements made no sense. Everyone assumed that he was crazy. Later on, he claimed that he had been hired to kill the pope by three men from Bulgaria, a Communist country in Eastern Europe. Some people believed that John Paul II's campaign for human rights had angered the Communists so much that they decided to silence him for good. The police never found the Bulgarians Ali Agca told them about, and they were never able to solve the mystery.

On Christmas Day, 1983, Pope John Paul II had a private meeting with Ali Agca in his prison cell. Although few Catholics around the world were prepared to forgive the gunman, John

Paul II heard Ali Agca's confession and gave him his personal forgiveness. Pierced by two bullets, the pope had demonstrated his faith by placing himself in the hands of the Virgin Mary. By pardoning the man who had tried to kill him, he was making a deliberate choice to forgive evil, following the example of Jesus.

When he returned to his normal activities, the pope understood that he would have to take precautions. Vatican security people fitted the popemobile with a bulletproof glass covering. The pope could still be seen by the people and could still give them his blessing. For the sake of safety, however, he could no longer mingle with crowds as he had enjoyed doing before.

When he resumed his world travels, John Paul II was as outspoken as ever. In 1983 he made a trip to Poland and threw his support behind the popular Solidarity movement, which had been banned by the Communist government. When he visited non-Communist countries in Western Europe and North America, he criticized them for caring too much about money and possessions. John Paul II condemned big businesses that treated workers as things rather than as people. He urged people not to make the mistake of thinking that everything was for sale, even honesty, loyalty, and love. In his view, religious faith could provide solutions where political systems failed. He meant to speak up for that faith, no matter what dangers he might face.

John Paul II gives his traditional Christmas blessing to the crowd in St. Peter's Square in 1983. Even though some Catholics believe that the pope is too conservative on religious issues, he continues to enjoy great popularity.

6

Holding Firm

In addition to promoting human rights, John Paul II has tried to bring Catholicism back to its roots. When he became pope, John Paul II believed that modern life was drawing people away from the church. It was time, he thought, for a return to traditional Catholic values. He has written, "The church guards the freedom of each individual who deliberately chooses God and wants to belong to Him." John Paul II has condemned what he believes are wrong directions in Catholics' thinking.

He has opposed such ideas as the ordination of women as priests, nuns giving up their religious dress for ordinary street clothes, and priests being allowed to marry.

Many Catholics disagree with the pope's ideas on these and other subjects. Even though they admire the pope and agree with his views on human rights, they argue that the church can do more if it changes with the times. They believe, for example, that young men will no longer choose to become priests unless the church allows them to marry and have families. The pope and those who agree with him insist that the church can do best by following the ideas that have worked for 2,000 years.

The pope has repeatedly condemned open criticism of church teachings. The Vatican has come down heavily on Catholic theologians who disagree with church doctrine, often causing them to lose their teaching jobs in Catholic schools. In 1986 the Catholic archbishop of Seattle, Washington, was punished for differing with Rome. These actions have angered some American Catholics in particular because Americans believe so strongly in freedom of speech, the right to say whatever one thinks. What happened, they wondered, to the openness of Cardinal Wojtyła when he became Pope John Paul II?

As pope, John Paul II had clearly decided to play the role of the strict father. (The Italian word for pope, *papa*, also means "father.") In his view, all Catholics must obey the teachings of their church as they would obey their parents, even if they disagree.

Despite criticism, the pope continued to speak out on political issues. On February 19, 1988, he published an *encyclical* called *On the Social Concerns of the Church*. (An encyclical is an open letter written by the pope for the instruction of Catholics.) In the encyclical he harshly criticized the larger and wealthier nations—especially the United States and the Soviet Union

John Paul II meets with Soviet leader Mikhail Gorbachev at the Vatican in December 1989. The pope has used his moral influence to promote world peace.

—for taking advantage of smaller, poorer countries. He then proposed a number of ideas for improving the world situation. His deepest hopes, he told a reporter just before the encyclical was published, were that nations could reach "brotherly understanding" and that individuals could be helped to grow "according to God's plan."

Because John Paul II's encyclical condemned the Communists and their opponents alike, both sides were offended by the document. After almost 10 years as pope, John Paul was clearly determined to speak out on political issues, whether or not his ideas were popular. In 1990, John Paul strongly condemned the Iraqi leader Saddam Hussein for invading the nation of Kuwait and thereby touching off a destructive war in the Persian Gulf. As Communist regimes began to fall in Eastern Europe, the pope voiced his full support for democratic parties and made a personal visit to Hungary. He did not gloat over the fall of communism, the church's longtime enemy.

Instead, he stated that the church had a special mission in the newly liberated nations: Eastern Europe must adopt spiritual values and avoid the love of money and possessions so common in the wealthier nations.

However much he concerns himself with world affairs, Pope John Paul II has never forgotten his Polish roots. He returned to Poland in 1991, after the triumph of the Solidarity movement. Solidarity's leader, Lech Walesa, a man John Paul had long supported, had been elected president of a democratic Poland. On World Youth Day, August 14, more than 1 million young people assembled for a celebration near the Shrine of the Black Madonna at Czestochowa (CHEN-sto-HO-vuh), Poland. The Black Madonna, depicted in a 1,500-year-old painting, is a cherished symbol of faith and endurance to Poles. John Paul II, recalling his lifelong love of his native country's mountains, told the crowd: "It is necessary for you to enter the big trails of

Lech Walesa, the leader of Poland's Solidarity movement, receives Holy Communion from John Paul II in 1987. Walesa's election as president of Poland in 1990 was also a triumph for the pope, who had long supported the democratic cause in his native land.

history, not only here in Europe but also on all continents, and to become, wherever they are, the witnesses to Christ's blessings. For what is at stake is the future, and the future is yours, young people."

Further Reading

Other Biographies of John Paul II

Bonic, Thomas. *His Holiness Pope John Paul II.*
    Toronto: Grolier, 1984.

Douglass, Robert W. *John Paul II, the Pilgrim Pope.*
    Chicago: Children's Press, 1980.

The Pope in America. Secaucus, NJ: Chartwell Books,
    1979.

Pope John Paul II Visits America. New York: Crescent
    Books, 1987.

Spink, Kathryn. *John Paul II in the Service of Love.*
    New York: Mayflower Books, 1978.

Related Books

Sandak, Cass R. *Poland.* New York: Watts, 1986.

Chronology

May 18, 1920	Karol ("Lolek") Wojtyła born in Wadowice, Poland
April 1929	Karol's mother, Emilia, dies in childbirth
Nov. 1932	Karol's brother, Edmund, dies of scarlet fever
1938	The Wojtyłas move to Kraków; Karol enrolls in the Jagellonian University
Sept. 1, 1939	Germany invades Poland; World War II begins
Feb. 1941	Karol's father dies
1945	The Soviet Union occupies Poland
1946	Wojtyła ordained a priest
1958	Named auxiliary bishop of Kraków
1962	Travels to Rome; attends Second Vatican Council
Jan. 1964	Named archbishop of Kraków
May 1967	Elevated to cardinal

Sept. 1978	Pope John Paul I dies
Oct. 16, 1978	John Paul II elected pope
1979	Tours Latin America, United States, and Poland
May 13, 1981	Survives St. Peter's Square assassination attempt
1983	Visits Poland; praises Solidarity
1987	Returns to United States and then Poland
1988	Publishes *On the Social Concerns of the Church*
May 2, 1991	Publishes *The Hundredth Year*
Aug. 14, 1991	On World Youth Day addresses 1 million people in Czestochowa, Poland, at the Shrine of the Black Madonna

Glossary

atheist   a person who denies the existence of God

bishop   in the **Roman Catholic church,** an official who ranks above a priest and who is usually in charge of a church district

blitzkrieg   a German word meaning "lightning war"; that is, a war conducted with great speed and force

cardinal   a high official of the Roman Catholic church, outranked only by the **pope**

Communist party   from 1945 to 1989 the ruling party of Poland that denied the existence of God but allowed Catholics to practice their religion

encyclical   an open letter from the pope to the members of the Roman Catholic church

excommunicate   to exclude a person from the rites and membership of a church

intellectual   an intelligent, educated, and creative person

papacy   the office of pope; also the term of a pope's reign

pope   the head of the Roman Catholic church

Roman Catholic church   the religion that follows the teachings of Jesus Christ and that is governed by the pope; its public worship centers around the Mass

seminary   a school or college for training priests, ministers, or rabbis

Solidarity   the workers' union formed in Poland that called for better working conditions and benefits for the working class

theology   the study of religion

Vatican   the official residence of the pope and the headquarters of the Roman Catholic church, located in Vatican City, within the city of Rome, Italy

Index

Jay Wilson received his bachelor's and doctoral degrees from Yale University. He has taught at the University of Rochester and is the author of biographical studies of St. Thomas More and his contemporaries. He is a student in the theology program at the St. John Neumann Residence in Riverdale, New York, and currently resides in Sarasota, Florida.

Picture Credits